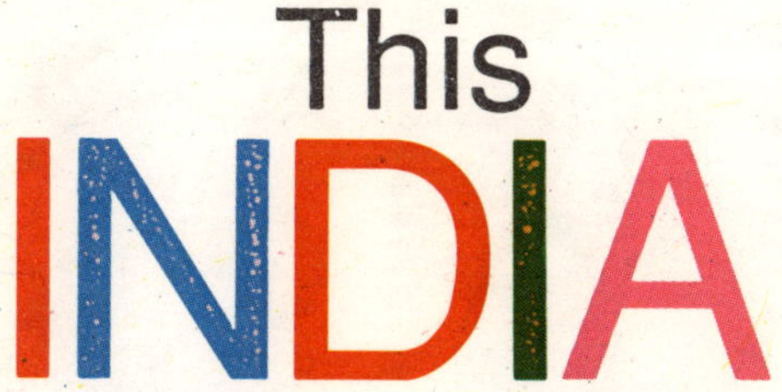
This INDIA

This
INDIA

Shahana Dasgupta

DESIGNED BY
Pankaj Goel

Rupa & Co

A Rupa Original
First Published 1993 by

Rupa & Co.
7/16, Ansari Road, Daryaganj, New Delhi - 110 002
15, Bankim Chatterjee Street, Calcutta- 700 073
135, South Malaka, Allahabad-211 001
P.G. Solanki Path, Lamington Road, Bombay - 400 007

Typeset in 12/14 pts. Garamond by
Quick Photocomposers
2-E, Rani Jhansi Road
New Delhi - 110 055

Photographs by Shashi Sahai
Illustrations by Irfan Hussain and Pankaj Goel

ISBN 81-7167-159-4
Rs. 145

Printed in India by
Gopsons Papers Pvt. Ltd.
A-28, Sector IX
Noida 201 301

To my parents

Contents

1 We Indians

2 Our Past

3 Our Present

Centrespread map of India with states and union territories.

4 Something to be proud of

5 Conclusion

6 Some Indians this Century.

श्रीलक्ष्मी नारायण श्रीगंगा जी
हरि नारायण जी का मन्दिर

We Indians

Mansur lives in Kashmir, the northern-most state in our country. It is spring in the Kashmir Valley and there are flowers everywhere — mustard flowers and crocuses and flowering fruit trees — in all kinds of beautiful colours. The winter has been long, cold and snowy; and Mansur is glad that the best part of the year has finally begun. This means that he can now spend time playing in the meadows and climbing up the apple trees in the orchards.

Mansur's father is a craftsman. He is one of the thousands of Kashmiris who make the woollen shawls which are so famous all over India and abroad. It takes him months to weave and embroider the shawls because it is difficult work and requires a lot of concentration. However, Mansur's father is a very skilful craftsman and his family has been making Pashmina shawls for many generations now. That is why he uses motifs for his shawls, which are hundreds of years old. Mansur does not go to school anymore. Instead, his father is teaching him how to weave so that one day he can carry on the family tradition. Most of his relatives are also craftsmen and they make carpets, or carve the wood of the walnut tree. There is a great demand for such handicrafts and Mansur's family is much better off today than his relatives were in the past.

Mansur and his family live in a wooden houseboat on one of Kashmir's many canals. Water is something that he has grown up with, and he does not find it at all unusual that he rarely gets to feel firm soil under his feet! In Kashmir, most business is carried on through the waterways and Mansur very often goes shopping by boat. The shops open right onto the water, so he simply rows his boat into them. Today his mother is busy washing clothes at the water's edge and his father has taken some of the shawls to a merchant. Mansur has to take care of his younger brother and sister, a task he does not particularly like. But this afternoon he is in a good mood as he watches the sunlight playing on the water and dreams of the future.

John

John comes from Kerala. Perhaps you have heard about, or seen photographs of Kerala, for it is one of our country's most beautiful states. Today being a workday, the villagers are busy in the fields or at

People in Kerala take part with much gusto and fanfare in the boat-racing festival of Onam. (Above)

John is a boy from the lush green landscapes and vast sand beaches of Kerala. (Facing page)

home and most of the children are at the village school. John's schoolteacher has been telling the class about Kerala's past. Kerala is somewhat separated from the rest of the country by the Western Ghats, so the people kept in touch with others more through their ports. Foreigners from Asia and Europe went to trade with the people in Kerala and they learnt a lot from each other.

Many religions came to Kerala as a result of this contact with foreigners, amongst them Christianity, which came many hundreds of years ago. Today many villagers are Christians, like John. Although most people are still Hindus, people of all religions, including Jews who were thrown out of other countries, manage to live together quite peacefully.

John's teacher has been telling the children that foreigners still travel to Kerala to admire the beaches, mountains, lakes and canals. In the olden days, they came to buy the spices and wood for which Kerala was famous. In fact, people in Kerala still grow pepper, cardamom, turmeric and ginger, along with coconuts, coffee and even tea! A lot of seafish and wood is sold abroad and the forests here still have some of the most expensive wood in the world.

John likes going to school and so do most of his friends in the village. He wants to study hard and become an engineer. Then he could work for some time in the Gulf countries and earn a lot of money. There are

many in the village like John's uncle, who had gone to Dubai or Kuwait to work. However, they all came back after a couple of years, and they have helped improve the village in many ways. In fact villages in Kerala are not like those in other parts of our country, because there is hardly any difference between them and the towns.

Kerala has plenty of water and most people travel from one place to another by boat. John has a friend whose father is a boatman. He has promised to take both the boys for a short trip down the river. Men like him spend a lot of time on their boats, on which they carry bananas and coconuts, and also ferry people across the rivers. John loves to sail down the peaceful blue water surrounded by thick coconut groves. The people in his village lead a life which is slow and close to the earth, and John himself feels that it is the earth and the water that best symbolize Kerala.

Tara

In the western part of our country is the state of Gujarat. It has fertile plains, the sea and vast areas of arid, treeless terrain. Here, in this land of contrasts, lives Tara. She has been very busy recently because her elder sister will be getting married soon. Tara has been helping her mother and aunts sew and embroider all her sister's clothes, as well as the quilts and bags that she will take with her as her dowry. Actually,

Tara's mother is a skilled craftswoman. Gujarati craftworks are very famous for their beautiful workmanship and vivid colours (Above)

Tara is a girl from the land of Dandiya Raas, Gujarat. (Facing page)

the women of the house start sewing these clothes many years before a wedding, because it takes so long to make each beautiful piece. For the last few days the women have been sitting together, singing and chatting as they stitch the colourful clothes.

Tara does not have much spare time though, for sewing. There is a lot of work to be done around the house, apart from the cooking and cleaning. Tara's mother is a good cook and the vegetarian food that she makes is delicious! Her father is a farmer. He has a plot of land, which, however small it may be, is his own. This could not have happened a few decades ago. However, re-distribution of land after our country's independence as well as the formation of cooperatives by farmers, in order to better their position, has made it possible for people like Tara's father to become small but successful farmers. Her brothers help in the fields and also spend a lot of time looking after the family's cattle and goats. Some of Tara's relatives live in towns and work in the textile factories, or own small shops. Gujaratis are skilful businessmen and Tara's cousins are doing quite well.

One of Tara's regular jobs is to go with her mother to the village well, in order to get water for the whole family. Both spend quite a long time talking to the other women as they await their turn to draw water. Today, there is a lot of discussion about the coming wedding. As Tara walks back home, carefully balancing the brass pot on her head, her mind too is on the wedding and how much fun it will be!

Abong

Abong lives in the thick jungles of Assam, which is the home of many tribal people. Some among them were the original inhabitants who lived in our country before all the others came, and many of them still live in the same way as they used to hundreds of years ago. The way Abong dresses and the language she speaks is very different from that of the other people in Assam.

Abong's parents, like most other tribals, are farmers. Apart from their own small vegetable garden, they grow a lot of fruit like pineapples and oranges. Almost every week, Abong walks with her parents to the nearest market, which is about 12 miles away, in order to sell the vegetables and fruit. It is a long and extremely tiring walk, but she enjoys the trip because of the many noises, the colours and the people. If her parents are in a good mood, they even buy her some necklaces or nose-rings. Abong is very fond of ornaments! At the market, there are non-tribal people who sell cloth and cheap plastic goods. However, traditional families like Abong's have their own loom, on which they weave all the cloth they need. So, Abong's mother mostly buys thread for weaving, pots and food for the family, while her father buys the tools he needs for his work. After all the buying and selling is over they gather at the tea stall owned by Abong's aunt. There are many such

Abong is a girl from the dense jungles of Assam. (Facing page)

Tea from the vast tea gardens of Assam is famous the worldover for its rich and unique flavour. (Above)

stalls at the marketplace, where people can drink a hot cup of tea after their day's work is done. Abong's aunt is very careful about cleanliness and she always dips each cup into boiling water before pouring tea into it. Abong and her parents then spend the rest of the time enjoying themselves, before beginning the long walk home.

Today, the villagers have met to celebrate the harvest. It has been good this year, which means that after many months of hard work, the people can finally relax. The women, in their bright red and black dresses, are singing about the harvest, and soon the dancing will start. The village priest has just arived after praying to the tribal gods and goddesses and thanking them for being generous. Abong loves the harvest festival because everybody forgets daily problems and is in a joyous mood. Over the meal, the villagers share jokes and the ones they find most funny are those about themselves! And so the merry-making continues late into the night.

Though town and city life have disturbed the way of life of Abong's people, the jungles still provide them with almost everything they need. Abong has never seen any other place but her own village and the market. She does not mind this very much and is quite happy living in her small village surrounded by her own people.

Mansur, John, Tara and Abong are children coming from the four corners of our country. They look different, they speak different languages and believe in different religions. Mansur is surrounded by mountains and snow, while Tara has the desert around her, John has grown up with rivers and lakes, while Abong has seen dense jungles and wildlife as long as she can remember.

You may well ask what do Mansur, John, Tara and Abong have in common, when so many important things in their lives are different? In fact, you may say, they might as well have come from different countries. Yes, India is a vast land with mountains and rivers, deserts and jungles. It also has every imaginable type of climate, from cold and snowy in the north, to hot and humid in the south and in the coastal areas. Some parts of our country get very little rainfall and are swept by dry and dusty winds for most of the year, while other regions are blessed by the monsoon rains. And just as varied as the landscape are its people. Yet, all of them have one very important thing in common — their being Indian. People from other parts of the world have come to our country at various times and have settled here. Their cultures, languages and religions have been tolerated and absorbed by those already living here, thus producing a unique mixture of people and ways of life, which make us one nation. All of us share this common heritage and this common past. And in the same way, whichever part of the country we come from, we have decided to share the same future. Mansur, John, Tara and Abong, all dream of a better and happier life in the land they live in.

This is the bust of a man who was, most probably, a priest. Notice his special garment. It is decorated with three-lobed forms called trefoils. Each trefoil was originally filled with a red paste. (Overleaf)

This is a house typical of Indus Valley Civilization. Notice the niches in the wall, similar to those still found in the houses and huts of Indian villages. Also notice the salinity at the floor level. (Overleaf)

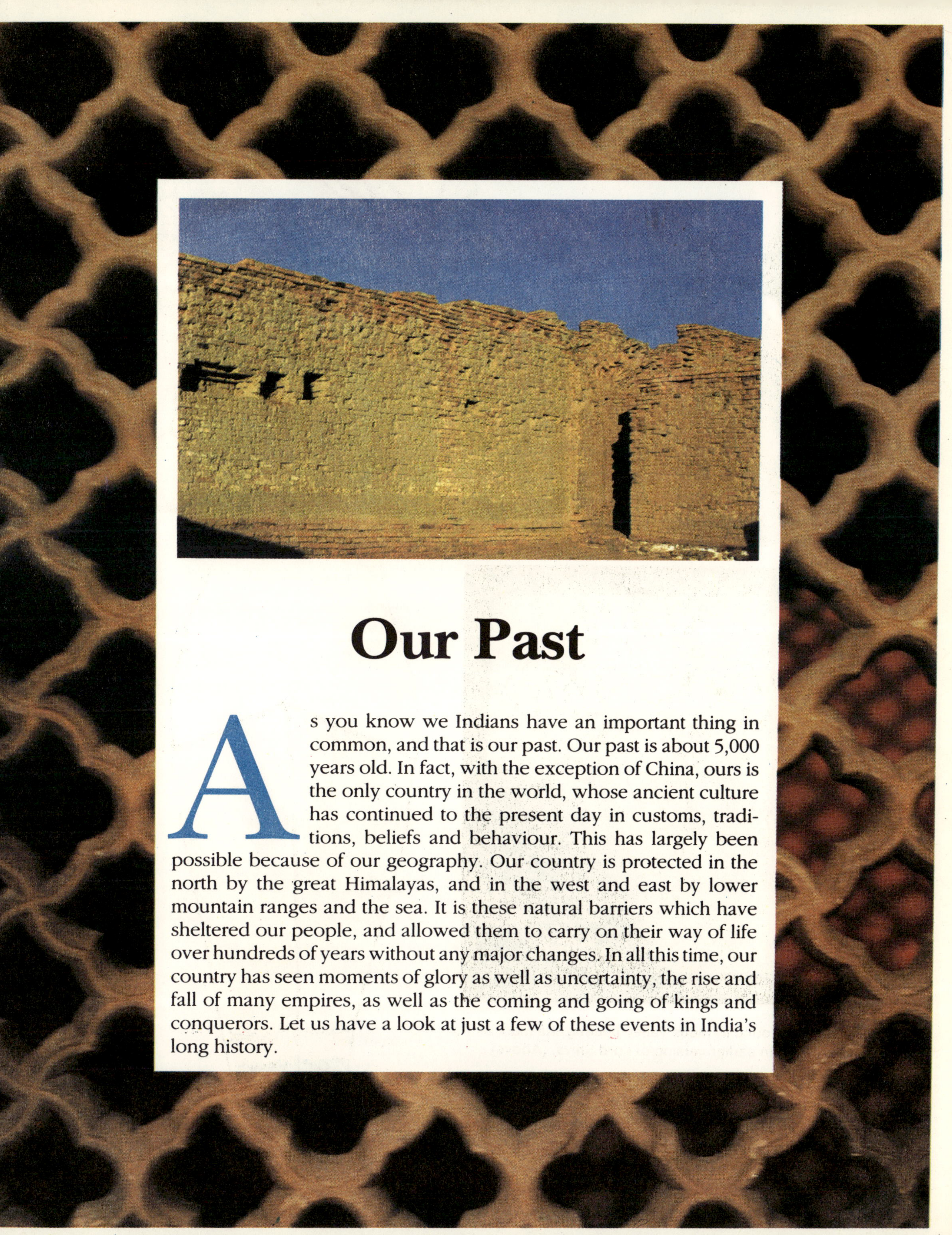

Our Past

As you know we Indians have an important thing in common, and that is our past. Our past is about 5,000 years old. In fact, with the exception of China, ours is the only country in the world, whose ancient culture has continued to the present day in customs, traditions, beliefs and behaviour. This has largely been possible because of our geography. Our country is protected in the north by the great Himalayas, and in the west and east by lower mountain ranges and the sea. It is these natural barriers which have sheltered our people, and allowed them to carry on their way of life over hundreds of years without any major changes. In all this time, our country has seen moments of glory as well as uncertainty, the rise and fall of many empires, as well as the coming and going of kings and conquerors. Let us have a look at just a few of these events in India's long history.

A dancing girl, so beaufifully captured in bronze. (Below)

This is a seal found in Indus Valley bearing the mark of Pashupati — an earlier version of Lord Shiva. (Above)

This seven inches high terracotta figurine dates from third or second century BC. Numerous such figures have been found in the north-western region of India. They are, almost certainly, variations of Mother Goddess or fertility — cult figures. (Right)

Indus Valley Civilization

Man had been existing in our country for many thousands of years before the Indus Valley Civilization, but when we Indians talk about our ancient culture we refer to people who lived in the Indus Valley, about 5,000 years ago. Excavations at Mohenjodaro in Sind and at Harappa in Punjab, both now in Pakistan, have revealed that this civilization existed not only in those areas but extended over Rajasthan and other parts of north India too. But exactly how far they extended has not yet been established. From the objects found at the various sites, we know that there was a link between the religion of these people and Hinduism. Unfortunately, the script on the seals found at the sites has not yet been deciphered, otherwise we would have known much more about this civilization. However, there is no doubt that theirs was a highly developed society and the people lived in well-planned cities, although they were engaged in some agriculture as well. Many of them were artists, merchants and farmers. The people wore clothes made of cotton and wool, liked beautiful ornaments and were fond of arts and crafts.

Stories of the wealth and riches of the Indus Valley Civilization became known to others, so it is not surprising that the Aryans invaded from the west. The Aryans were an energetic people. They had better weapons and were good horsemen. In fact, it was they who introduced the horse and the chariot into the country. In the battles that followed, many citizens of Mohenjodaro and Harappa were killed and the rest managed to escape to the south of our country. Thus a great civilization came to an end.

The Aryans

The Aryans first came to India around 1500 B.C. and they continued to come over many centuries. They originally settled in the Punjab and later on spread over the Indo-Gangetic plain. Unlike the inhabitants of the Indus Valley they were a nomadic people who did not know how to live in cities. So they settled in little villages. Amongst them were farmers, weavers, carpenters and blacksmiths. Each tribe had a king and soldiers. There were priests as well, who slowly became more and more powerful.

So the tribes formed into kingdoms. Their culture and society slowly developed to form the Hindu heritage, which we are so proud of today. However, one bad aspect of Hindu society had its roots in this period of our history. This was the caste system, which in the beginning was not very strict. People were originally divided according to their professions and occupations. And there used to be a good deal of free movement from one group to another. But gradually things changed - when and how no one knows for certain. Four main castes emerged. The highest caste was that of the priest, then came the warrior, the

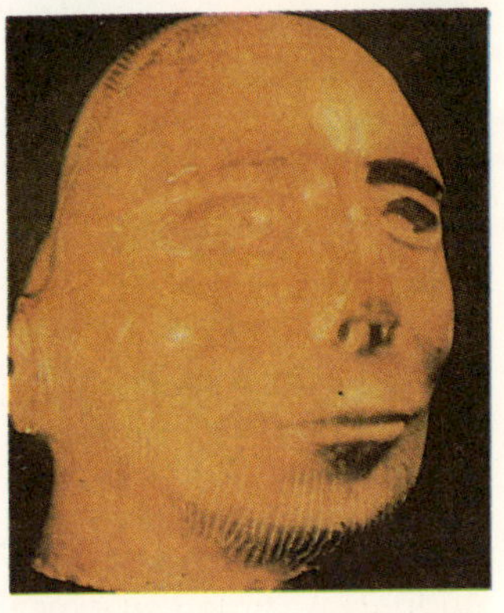

This is the head of a man of aristocratic bearing. Those ancient people had a very firm division of people into classes. (Above)

The dice along with this chess-set makes it unusual, does it not? (Top)

merchant and finally the serf. Over the years, a new category was formed. That of the untouchables and they were below all the other castes. With time, the upper castes took away more and more rights from the lower castes. The position of the untouchables became especially bad. Men like Buddha, and later on, Mahatma Gandhi, tried to show how inhuman the system had become.

Ashoka

More and more Aryan kingdoms spread across the Gangetic plain at the expense of independent tribal organizations. Such were the kingdoms of Magadha, Kausambi, Kosala and Avanti during the sixth century B.C. It was at this time that many began to be dissatisfied with the way the Hindu religion was being practised. The message conveyed by Buddhism and Jainism, therefore, found a ready response among the people. There was religious discontent, but people were not otherwise unhappy with their daily lives. This was the state of affairs when from far away Greece, Alexander the Great came right up to the river Beas in 330 B.C. He defeated the local chiefs and brought this area of Punjab under his control. But after his death, Chandragupta Maurya defeated the Greeks whom Alexander had left behind. Guided

by his counsellor Chanakya he attacked the Nandas, the ruling dynasty of the kingdom of Magadha and became the ruler of Magadha. Young Chandragupta, together with Chanakya, then set out to create the first empire in India. This extended from the Indus in the west to the Brahmaputra in the east, from the Himalayas in the north to the Vindhyas in the south. During the 24-year reign of Chandragupta

Maurya, an efficient administrative and revenue system was set up, importance was given to irrigation and transport, and a well-organized network of police and spies was developed. Although peace and prosperity was brought to the country by a number of rulers, one emperor stood above all the rest.

Ashoka was perhaps the greatest of all Indian rulers. He became emperor in 321 B.C. To expand his empire, he fought a war with the Kalingas, in which thousands died and many more were injured. Ashoka was filled with sadness at the sight of so much suffering and he decided to give up warfare altogether. His mind turned towards Buddha's teachings of compassion and love. Missionaries were sent to faraway places like Syria, Egypt and Greece. It was Ashoka, who by sending his brother and later on his sister, as royal missionaries, took Buddhism to Sri Lanka. Ashoka saw that through tolerance and peaceful, non-violent methods he could win over neighbouring kings. He called his subjects his children and did a lot for the well-being of his people. Ashoka also built stupas and pillars with inscriptions, which not only have artistic value, but from which we have come to know a lot about life during his reign. The lion-column, which is now the national symbol of our country, was built at this time.

The Period of the Guptas

After the death of Ashoka, the Mauryan dynasty lasted another hundred years before the empire disappeared. Then followed a period when northern India was ruled by various kings and subjected to attacks by tribes from the north-west. It was around 320 A.D. that once again a glorious dynasty established itself, and the 200 years of Gupta rule saw achievements in various directions.

To begin with, the Guptas developed trade with the Mediterranean countries, alongside the traditional contacts with the East. This led to prosperity in the country, which could be seen in the way of life of the people. For instance, there was a lot of interest in art and architecture and some impressive Hindu temples were built at this time. This period not only saw Sanskrit literature reach a state of perfection, but there was an interest in philosophy as well. The achievements in science were no less impressive. The concept of the zero in mathematics, as well as the theory of the decimal system, were discoveries which took place at this time, and they completely changed the world of mathematics and science. Two great scientists Aryabhata and Varahamira also lived during this age.

The Gupta period is known as the Golden Age of Hinduism. Hinduism was reorganized and its message brought closer to the people. The *Mahabharata*, the great epic of the Hindus, was edited and put together in a new form at this time. It is this version that has been handed down to us. However, despite the great revival of

Sanchi Stupa
(Facing page)

Hinduism, Buddhism remained an important religion and many scholars from other countries came to study at the university of Nalanda in Bihar.

Harsha

The Gupta empire broke up into various kingdoms around the sixth century A.D. It was not until the arrival of Harsha in the beginning of the seventh century A.D. that north India, once again, came under the authority of one person. Harsha's empire was made up of independent kingdoms, which accepted him as their emperor. We have a very detailed record of life during Harsha's time from the descriptions of the Chinese traveller and pilgrim Huien Tsang. Also, the *Harsha Charita*, written by Bana, contains a lot of information about Harsha's reign. Harsha himself, was a writer and poet and interested in the arts, but at the same time, he did not neglect his duties as emperor. Although a Buddhist, he maintained strong links with Hinduism, even praying to Shiva. The 41 years of Harsha's reign were indeed, an important period in our country's history. Thereafter, the empire broke up once again into various kingdoms, and a new element in the shape of Islam entered the country, to become a part of our culture and civilization.

The Arrival of the Muslims

Just before the reign of Harsha, the Huns had for some time established themselves in north-west India. However, their rule did not last long. Yet the attempts thereafter by the Muslims to establish themselves beyond Sind, remained largely unsuccessful, though elsewhere they spread through much of the world. Within India itself, from the 7th to the 11th centuries, the long years of peace and stability resulted in a feeling amongst the people, that they were beyond the reach of any enemy. So their armies had become weak. An equally important development arising from the many centuries of peace, was a sense of complacency and isolation, as a result of which society too had become decadent. People lacked the new ideas that often come from contact with the outside world. It was, therefore, no surprise, that when eventually the better organized Muslims made a determined attempt to conquer the Gangetic valley, they were able to overcome all resistance.

It did not take Mohammed Ghori and his governor Qutbuddin Aibak, very long to establish an empire, which included the Punjab, Gangetic plain and Bengal, with its capital at Delhi. On Mohammed Ghori's death in 1206, Qutbuddin Aibak became Sultan and established the first dynasty of the Delhi Sultanate. He was followed by Iltutmish, who is also remembered for having completed the famous Qutab Minar in Delhi. The dynasty included a capable Queen, Raziya, who, however, met with considerable opposition because she was a woman. The first dynasty of the Delhi Sultanate had to give way to the next, when the Khaljis came to power. Amongst them, Alauddin Khalji is remembered as being the most outstanding. He extended the Delhi Sultanate. After his death there was a period of chaos until a new dynasty - the Tughlaqs - came to power in 1320 A.D. But they too were not able to keep the conquered territories together. You have probably heard of the mad king Mohammad-bin-Tughlaq, whose policies resulted in the final break-up of the Delhi Sultanante. So at the end of the 14th century, taking advantage of the weak Delhi Sultanate, the brutal Amir Timur easily plundered the city of Delhi and massacred its inhabitants. After this terrible invasion, the only dynasty of any importance to rule from Delhi, were the Lodhis, but they were unable to restore the Delhi Sultanate to its past importance, and Delhi and northern India lay open to a new invader.

The Mughuls

In 1526, the Delhi Sultanate fell to the armies led by Babar, and a new dynasty called the Mughuls came to power. They were Muslims from Central Asia and they were to rule for nearly 200 years. When Babar died in 1530, he had succeeded in establishing control over Delhi and the territories of the Lodhis. He was followed by his son Humayun, who was a man of culture, but not much of a soldier. In the process of expanding the Mughul territories he met with resistance from Sher Shah from the east, and had to spend 15 years in exile in Persia. As a result, the Mughuls from then onwards, came under a strong Persian influence.

In 1556,Humayun was succeeded by his young son Akbar. In 1562, when he was only 22 years old, he married a Hindu princess and so won the support of the Hindus. When he died the empire stretched from Afghanistan in the west, to Bengal in the east. Akbar was very interested in religion and philosophy and held many discussions with learned men of all religions. He was the greatest of the Mughul rulers and the prestige and power of India grew with him. Even after his death, our country continued to occupy a leading position in the world.

Akbar's son Jehangir, generally followed the policies of his father. Although he was a devout Muslim, he showed a deep interest in other religions. Jehangir's life and reign was strongly influenced by his Persian wife Noor Jehan. She was not only a woman of great beauty but also intelligent, ambitious and cultured. Due to her, the Mughul court became even more influenced by Persian traditions.

Shah Jehan who succeeded his father Jehangir, kept the Mughul empire more or less intact. It is not so much for his qualities as a soldier or ruler that he is remembered, but for the splendour of his court and the beautiful buildings that he created. The Red Fort and the Jama Masjid in Delhi, the Moti Masjid in Agra and, of course, the magnificent

Taj Mahal. This famous monument, which symbolizes India all over the world, was built as a tomb for his beloved wife, Mumtaz Mahal.

Aurangzeb deposed his father, Shah Jahan, and inherited an empire, which he extended even further. He was a good soldier and administrator and could have carried on the glory of the Mughuls. Unfortunately, he sowed the seeds that led to its destruction. Aurangzeb was an orthodox Muslim and he wanted to create an Islamic state. He lost the support which the Hindus had given the Mughuls since Akbar. He also faced strong opposition from the Marathas under Shivaji in the south and the Sikhs under Guru Gobind Singh in the north. Thus, it was with Aurangzeb that the down fall of the Mughul empire began.

The Mughul period is remembered for a number of reasons. Literature, painting and music reached a high degree of excellence. The great poet Tulsidas wrote his *Ramacharitamanas* during this time. The Mughuls also built some of the most beautiful palaces and monuments in our country. The courts of the Mughul emperors were famous for their magnificence and splendour. India was a prosperous country at this time and the common man lived in comfort.

South India

Before we take a look at India's more recent history, let us see what was happening in other parts of the country. We know that the Mauryas maintained friendly relations with the three southern kingdoms of Chola, Pandya and Chera. In the northern Deccan, the Satvahanas – a great dynasty — ruled for nearly 300 years, from 73 B.C. to 218 A.D. When their dynasty came to an end, they were succeeded, amongst others, by the Chalukyas and the Pallavas. These two great dynasties then controlled the history of South India for another 300 years.

The history of south India shows, that unlike in north India, society and culture were stable and unbroken. By the fifth century A.D., the great Pallava dynasty had started to rule, and they remained in power till the middle of the eighth century A.D. They built the famous temples of Mahabalipuram and were also patrons of literature. Their great city of Kanchi was a centre of learning and had a university, which equalled Nalanda in the north. Another important dynasty of about the same time was of the Chalukyas. Both these dynasties had a big navy and they kept in touch with countries like Malaya and Indonesia. In fact, Hindu influence can be seen even today, in names, dress and the arts of the people in those countries.

The Chola dynasty succeeded the Pallavas, and during the 400 years of their rule, many remarkable achievements took place in art and architecture. By the end of the 13th century A.D., this empire too broke up. In the meantime, the north had come into contact with the Muslims. The south, however, was able to defend itself against them for a long

Taj Mahal - one of the seven wonders. Built on the banks of river Yamuna in Agra, Taj Mahal is a tribute to the memory of Mumtaj Mahal, the Begum of Mughul Emperor Shahjahan. Its construction began in 1632 and took 22 years and labour of 20,000 men to be completed. (Facing page)

time, because the kingdoms there were politically more stable and the people were proud of their monarchs.

The disintegration of the Chola dynasty in the 13th century A.D. gave the Muslims a chance to attack the south, but they could not establish themselves. This was mainly due to the Vijayanagar dynasty. Its greatest king was Krishnadeva Raya, who ruled in the 16th century A.D. He was a wise king and a good soldier, and the people lived in prosperity under him. However, in the end, the south too came under the Muslims. One must mention that the Vijayanagar empire had been in constant conflict with the Bahamanis—a Muslim dynasty which had established itself in the area north of the Krishna river in 1347. The kingdom existed till the end of the 15th century and then broke up into five states — Berar, Ahmednagar, Bijapur, Golconda and Bidar.

The Northeast

Assam, because of its geographical barriers, was able to keep its political independence for a long time, although it was no different, culturally and economically, from other parts of eastern India. It was also able to defend itself against the Muslims. However, in the 13th century, the groups living in Assam were attacked by tribesmen from Burma, who settled in the valley. Over the years, they became Hindus and dropped their own tribal language and started speaking the language of the people they had conquered. The whole area was, therefore, greatly influenced by the Hindu way of life. However, it was also a meeting place of Hindu and Mongolian ideas, the tribal people being of Mongolian origin.

The British

India remained a leading industrial country in the 16th, 17th and part of even the 18th century. It exported spices, textiles and glass, and was known for shipbuilding. Many European countries were very interested in maintaining good relations with India and trading with it. However, about the time the Mughuls came to power, the land routes to India, through which the Europeans carried on their trade, were blocked by the Turks. The Europeans tried to find a new route round the southern part of Africa, and finally in 1498, the Portuguese Vasco da Gama landed on the western coast of India. The Dutch, the English, the French and even the Danes, started using this sea route in order to trade with India. In the beginning, the Europeans only wanted to trade, and in any case, the Mughul empire was so powerful that they could not do much more. So, for two centuries, trade carried on quite peacefully. The Indians did not expect that anyone coming across the sea could pose a threat. But by the 18th century, the Mughul empire had become very weak. Also the Mughuls did not have a powerful navy. There were battles with the Marathas and the Sikhs and this caused the

Rani Jhansi — the great warrior queen. In the absence of her husband, she dared to lead her small army against the mighty forces of British. She sacrificed her life to the cause of freedom but still won the grudging respect of her opponents, the British. (Facing page)

breakup of the empire. In the meantime, a group of British merchants, known as the East India Company, had established themselves as the main trading power amongst the Europeans. Until then, a substantial amount of India's trade was still being chanelled through the land routes. It was the British, however, who not only monopolized all trade with India, but also made the sea route the only channel. India was thus cut off from all neighbouring countries in Asia and remained so, until we became independent in 1947.

The centre of British activity in India was Bengal. It was here that the British won the battle of Plassey in 1757, against Siraj-ud-Daula, the Nawab of Bengal. This victory is said to have marked the beginning of British military power in our country. The British saw their chance in the confusion caused by civil war, and took it. The East India Company used its trading rights to influence local politics and thus slowly took over power in our country. One by one, the Deccan territories of the Marathas, Rajputana, and Punjab after the death of Ranjit Singh, all fell to the British. In the end, they were the supreme power in the country.

Of the many Governors -General who ruled India, two - William Bentinck and Dalhousie - were important. Bentinck's act of abolishing the terrible Hindu practice of sati, the burning of a widow on her husband's funeral pyre, was the first time that social reform of Hinduism was brought about by law. Dalhousie is known for expanding British power in India. He was also a capable administrator and he laid the first railway line, as well as the first telegraph lines in our country. We owe the construction of the Ganga canal and the modern Grand Trunk Road to him. He was also interested in social reform and education.

In 1857, the British received their first shock when Indian soldiers employed under them revolted. These soldiers were helped by the Mughul princes, Nana Sahib, the Rani of Jhansi and Tantia Tope. Although the British succeeded in putting down the rebellion, things were never quite the same again. In 1858, the Company was broken up by the British parliament and the British government started to rule India directly. As a result, the administration of the country, the development of railways, roads, and irrigation projects, was given importance, unlike the time the country was under the East India Company. Also, another Governor-General, Ripon, widened local and municipal self-government in 1882. Despite these changes, the British Government ruled India for its own benefit, so, our country, which had once been a big industrial nation, became poorer and poorer. The British purposely destroyed India's industry, so that Indians would not be able to produce their own goods and would be forced to buy British products. The arts and crafts of our country, which used to be famous all over the world, suffered very badly. Pressure on land increased tremendously, because more and more people began to live off agriculture. A rather gloomy period in our country's history had begun.

India Awakes

It took some time for our country to pull its forces together and to move forward once again. The man who first brought new ideas to Hindu religion and society was Raja Rammohun Roy. He wanted to do away with the caste system and, therefore, founded the Brahmo Samaj. Raja Rammohun Roy supported women's rights, argued against sati, and believed in the importance of education. Today, we Indians call ourselves a secular country. That means that in our country, we consider all religions to be equal. We owe it to Raja Rammohun Roy for starting the secular movement in India. Many say that he was "the first modern man in our country."

Men like Raja Rammohun Roy, Dayanand Saraswati, Ishwarchandra Vidyasagar, Ranade and Vivekananda, gave a new direction to Hinduism. Western political and economic ideas also had a great impact on the new generation of lawyers, doctors, journalists and teachers, who began to dream of a modern, united India, free from foreign rule. The British system of education introduced at that time, created modern universities and schools in India, and even today our country functions according to a legal system given to us by Macaulay. Many Englishmen contributed to the feeling of national pride amongst Indians. William Jones translated Kalidas' Sanskrit classic *Shakuntala*, and not only made the richness of Indian literature known to the West, but to Indians as well. James Princep deciphered the inscriptions on Ashoka's pillars and thereby made it possible to study ancient Indian history. It was British scholars who, together with other Europeans, researched Indian literature, art, philosophy and history, and made Indians aware of their rich and glorious past.

As national feeling grew, Indians demanded more political and economic rights. At this time, some Englishmen, particularly A.O. Hume, helped the Indians to form the Indian National Congress in 1885, so that they could voice these demands in an organized manner. The British had no idea that the Congress would challenge them one day. In the beginning, the demands for reform made by members of the Congress, such as Dadabhai Naoroji, Surendra Nath Banerjea and Gopal Krishna Gokhale, were quite moderate. However, some members began to get impatient with the slow changes that were taking place and wanted the British to leave India altogether. The leader of this more extremist group was Balgangadhar Tilak, who belonged to Pune. It was 'Lokmanya' Tilak, who first said "swaraj is my birthright." Some of the others who supported him were, Aurobindo Ghosh and Lala Lajpat Rai. Apart from these two groups, there was a third which believed that by planting bombs, or killing British officials, they could drive the British out of India. To this group belonged the

Savarkar brothers, Khudiram Bose and later on, Bhagat Singh.

The First World War took place from 1914 to 1918. Thousands of Indian soldiers died fighting for the British and huge sums of Indian money were used to support the British during the war. Yet, in 1919, the British, did not hesitate to take repressive measures against Indians. This came to be known as the Jallianwala Bagh tragedy. The British shot dead hundreds of unarmed Indians, who had come together in a park in Amritsar, to celebrate a festival. The tragedy shocked the Indians and after that there was no more support for the British in India. In 1920, Mahatma Gandhi started his non-violent struggle for independence, and soon all the people of India were taking part in the fight for freedom.

The Fight for Freedom

Mohandas Karamchand Gandhi was a person so unique that even a

Dandi March — carried out by Gandhiji as an act of protest, it sought to abolish the salt laws of the British. Gandhiji and his followers marched from Sabarmati to Dandi.

genius like the scientist Albert Einstein once said of him, that future generations will not believe that such a man ever walked the earth. Mahatma Gandhi was born in Porbander, in 1869. In 1888, he left to study law in England and after becoming a barrister, he went to work in South Aftrica. There, he saw the unfair way in which the South African government dealt with the Indian community. This made him think about using the unusual weapons of non-violence and non-cooperation, in order to obtain justice for the Indians. In 1915, he came back home and with his arrival, the days of the British in India

were numbered. **Mahatma Gandhi reunited the quarrelling members of the Indian National Congress.** Most importantly, he started to involve the vast masses of our countrymen who lived in the villages, in the freedom movement. There were other reasons too, especially, the worsening economic condition which made even the poorest farmer, whether in Bengal, Maharashtra, Uttar Pradesh or Tamil Nadu, join him in his fight against the British.

Mahatma Gandhi's heart belonged to the poor villagers of our country. He saw how helpless they were and how their lives had been ruined by British rule. He knew that in order to help them, he had to get rid of the British. Mahatma Gandhi fought the British with all peaceful and fair means possible, and thus won the respect of not only the British, but the whole world. In 1918, the British government had announced a set of reforms called the Montagu-Chelmsford reforms. Among other suggestions, the reforms called for more powers being given to the individual provinces, so that they could settle many administrative matters themselves. However, popular discontent continued. In 1927, the British, in order to calm down the Indians, announced the setting up of the Simon Commission, which was to advise the governement on how to set up a parliament and instal an elected government. But the Commission did not have any Indian members and this angered the people. They saw the reforms as "always too little, always too late," and demanded *purna swaraj* or total independence in 1929.

In 1930, Gandhi began his famous Dandi march, during which he intended to break the law by openly collecting salt from the sea. **Meanwhile, it was becoming clear that many Hindus and Muslims felt they could not participate in a unified national movement.** The Muslims feared that their interest would not be taken care of in a Hindu-dominated country. Thus, they increasingly placed their confidence in the Muslim League. The rising influence of purely Hindu parties, further complicated matters. Under Mohammad Ali Jinnah, the demand for a separate Muslim state became more powerful. And in 1940, this demand was incorporated in a resolution of the Muslim League. Meanwhile, in the Government of India Act of 1935, the British proposed the setting up of a federal form of government. Although a lot of authority was given to the provinces this was not considered enough by the Indians. In this atmosphere, the second World War broke out in 1939. Since the British were not interested in transferring real power to India at this time, the Congress governments which had assumed power in most provinces after the elections, resigned in protest. The Quit India Movement of 1942 was India's final answer to the British. All Congress leaders were immediately put in jail.

While Gandhi believed that Indians could make the British leave the country by refusing to cooperate with them in any way, there were men like Subhas Chandra Bose who wished that stronger and quicker action be taken. However, he was not very successful in getting others to agree with him. But Bose was a man of action and he was not prepared to wait while others argued over what to do. In 1941, he managed to leave the country and form the Indian National Army abroad, with the aim of throwing the British out with Japanese help. Though he was out of India, people knew about Bose from his speeches and articles, and had also heard about his courage and bravery. In the end, Subhas Chandra Bose's plans were unsuccessful, but his legend and his famous words *Jai Hind* still live on.

The second World War came to an end in 1945. The British started political negotiations with the released Congress leaders and on August 15, 1947, real power was finally transferred to a government led by the Congress. However, the country was partitioned with the creation of a new state of Pakistan.

Three of the leaders of the freedom movement — Jayaprakash Narayan, Jawaharlal Nehru and Sardar Patel — continued to dominate politics even after independence. J.P. Narayan came to be accepted as the true voice of Mahatma Gandhi, but he never joined the government. So, independent India was actually led by two men, Nehru and Patel. Patel was a very good organizer and administrator. Our country owes a great deal to him for solving many of its problems wisely. But he died soon after independence, and Nehru had to carry on the task of holding the country together and making up for the years of neglect and exploitation. Nehru was our country's first prime Minister. He came from a well-off family and was educated abroad. When he returned to India, he saw how poor and backward many of his countrymen were, and his love for them and his country made him want to do something about it. He knew that if India was to become strong and prosperous again, it had to stop being dependent on other countries for every small item from soap to needles. Not only would India have to make the little things itself, but would have to produce the iron and steel to make big machines, railway engines, cars and bicycles. This pressing task could only be undertaken by setting up factories all over the country, and by using India's rich natural resources, such as iron and coal deposits. The process of industrializing India was begun by Jawaharlal Nehru. He started the Five-Year Plans which put the country on the road to progress in many areas other than industry. He gave great importance to science and technology and thereby brought the atomic age to our country. Nehru also continued some of Mahatma Gandhi's goals such as giving women more rights. He had a special love for children and we celebrate his birthday as 'Children's Day'.

Our Tricolour. Every time it unfurls, it brings to our hearts a whole new gamut of hopes, promises and ambitions. A symbol of our pride, we are ever ready to sacrifice our lives to this glorious flag. (Overleaf)

Packets being unloaded from a truck. Industrialisation has brought about a whole new range of services, such as transportation, communications etc. This also means more employment for our countrymen. (Overleaf)

Our Present

The India that we have grown up in, and know so well, is a little over 46 years old today. The way we live and what we see around us is quite different from what it was when our parents were as old as us. While some things have changed for the better, others have not changed at all. Many of us live more comfortably than our parents did. But for many others, life is as bad as it was in the past, or maybe even worse. Although quite some time has passed since independence we are still a poor country. Indeed, many people around the world who do not know of our proud past, picture modern India as a dirty country full of people who are hungry, homeless and cannot read or write. They see how badly the scheduled castes are treated in our country and how we Hindus, Muslims and Sikhs fight amongst ourselves. We have to admit that all of this is partly true. Still, many positive things have happened in the recent past. Let us see what has been done and where we have to try harder.

If you are a Hindu, you know that you belong to some caste or the other. Not so very long ago, people from the higher castes were not allowed to come into contact with the untouchables, or scheduled castes as they are called. Nor were the untouchables allowed to use the same village well as the others, or enter the village temple. In this century, one of the main causes for which Mahatma Gandhi fought all his life was getting rid of untouchability and assuring the scheduled castes social equality and basic rights. Also, he wanted to give them the opportunities available to the upper castes, so that they too could one day occupy the well-paid influential jobs denied to them all along. Most Indians are poor, and most of these poor people belong to the scheduled castes and tribes who live in the villages. Gandhi's ideas have been put into action since independence, because we have come to realize that India cannot progress unless we get rid of the caste system. This is the burning issue today because whenever changes for

the better have been suggested or actually introduced these have met with strong opposition from social customs and ways of thinking. Much of this **orthodoxy** has come to be associated with India's major religions. So it is not always easy to move forward when a large number of people refuse to accept that not all traditions are good.

Big changes are nonetheless taking place in towns and cities. Caste is no longer so important, as people of all castes have to live and work together, travel in the same buses and shop in the same markets. Also people no longer have the occupations they would have by tradition. It is our villages which have not developed so fast, and there the caste system still exists, although there has been some change there too. For instance, many upper caste people in the villages today work at jobs they would not have taken up before, simply because they are better paid. Also, there are Brahmins who do manual work on their farms, which would have been unheard of in the past.

People realized that the scheduled castes, who form the majority of our country's poor, could lead better lives only if they owned the land they worked on. Therefore, soon after independence, the government decided to take land away from rich landowners, who did not work on their own land, and to give it to the extremely poor peasants instead. These land reforms are a beginning, though they have not always been successfully implemented for various reasons. But, at least they hold out the hope that the old, unjust system will disappear in the future.

Three-quarters of our population lives in the villages. At the time of independence, Nehru saw that one of our country's most valuable resources was its villagers, and he knew that their participation was necessary in the building of a new India. Since then, a lot of importance has been given to community development, so that poverty, disease and ignorance can be removed from the villages. Both the government and private organizations, have helped set up health services and village schools, build roads, dig wells and bring electricity to the countryside.

Though thousands of Indian villages still look very much like what they did in the past, a change has taken place. Today people in rural areas are more ready to accept new methods of farming, better seeds and to use fertilizers. But most of all, they want to know more about the world around them. Also, the way they think about things is very different from the past. There are also changes that you can see. For instance, there is a demand in our villages for cloth made in mills and not on the traditional handloom; for glasses and plates made of plastic and not clay and for watches and transistors. Many men wear shirts and trousers. So you see, in some ways, the countryside is becoming like the town or the city.

A country can modernize itself and progress if its people have some kind of basic education. The men who led our country after independence, realized the importance of education and made it compulsory for all children under the age of 14, to go to school. But, in reality, more than half our people cannot read or write and many children, especially in the villages, do not go to school at all. Try to imagine what would happen to you if you could not read or write. Would you be able to become what you wanted to be when you grew up? What would you do if somebody came and showed you something written on a piece of paper and forced you to agree to it, by making you put your thumb-mark on it? You would not know what you were agreeing to, and would simply have to believe whatever people told you. There would be some who would take advantage of you. This is what happens to millions of illiterate children when they grow up. Today, there are more children in the country who can read and write, than at the time of independence, but there are still millions of poor children who cannot. This is one of our country's biggest problems

– trying to see that all its people, especially those in the rural areas, have a minimum level of education.

When the British left India in 1947, there was not enough food and hardly any industries in the country. Everything we used came from abroad. On the other hand, the country was known to be rich in natural and mineral resources. Nehru saw that if India was to become a modern, industrial nation these resources would have to be developed. In order to raise the quality of life of the people, they had to be given adequate food, clothing, housing and health care. He knew very well that India did not have enough money or resources to go around. So he decided to introduce Five Year Plans to make proper use of our limited money and resources. This meant that the government would draw up a plan of all the things it wanted to achieve in five years. It would then assess the progress and see where the faults lay, before settling the next Five-Year Plan. We are now in the Eighth Plan. In the time covered by these eight plans the face of our country has changed quite a bit. Let us briefly see what has changed the most.

So far, ours has been an agricultural country. Most Indians live in villages and earn their living through agriculture. The first task that lay ahead was to grow more food and to make life a little better for the poor who lived in the villages. It was thought that if farmers were helped to grow more food, they could sell the extra food and make some money, and this food could then be used to feed the millions in our country. Therefore, the First Plan set about providing better seeds for irrigation. Until then, our farmers had been totally dependent on the rains for a good harvest, but with the building of huge dams like Bhakra, Hirakud and Tungabhadra, they were able to rely on a constant source of water for their crops. This huge programme, to grow more food, later on developed into the 'Green Revolution' when many parts of our country became prosperous, because farmers used the new techniques introduced by the government. Today, our country is self-sufficient in food and no major famines have taken place since independence. You may ask why, despite all this progress, so many people are still poor and hungry. Well, that is partly because land reforms have not been implemented properly in many parts of the country, with the result that the poor in the villages still have to go without many things that are available in the market. But the main reason why the poor in the villages have continued to be poor is that the Green Revolution has been successful only in some parts of the country and it is mostly the rich farmers who have been given the fertilizers, new seeds and irrigation facilities.

Apart from growing our own food, we also wanted to develop our industries. In today's modern world, we depend heavily on industries, and in order to become a strong country, we needed a sound industrial base. India is rich in mineral resources and has coal, iron, manganese,

An industrial worker — the basic building block of our modern society. (Above)

mica, bauxite, petroleum and a variety of metals. However, at the time of independence, we were using only a tiny portion of our vast mineral wealth. And not only that, whatever we produced was sent in its raw form to other countries. There, they would extract the metal from the ore and make expensive products out of it, whereas we only got the low prices obtained from selling the ore. Besides rich natural resources, our country now has enough skilled and educated workers, so there is no reason why we cannot become an industrial country. The problem lay in putting our resources together. Therefore, in the Second Five Year Plan, it was decided to find out what metals lay beneath the earth and where they could be found, and then to set up factories to purify the metal. Also the aim of the Second Plan was to increase steel production, develop the chemical industry and start making heavy machinery. Today, nearly 46 years later, India makes machines and many other industrial products. So, in a few decades, our country's scientists and engineers have brought in nuclear and electronic technology and put India firmly on the road to industrialization. The credit for much of this industrialization must go to government organizations. These form the public sector of our economy. Individual industrialists, who make up the private sector, have also done a good deal.

Although agriculture and industry were the focus of the first few five years plans, other areas such as education, health, housing, railways and roads were also covered. However, everything did not go exactly as we had planned. Sometimes there was a shortage of electricity, or coal production was low, or there was a drought in parts of the country. These, and other factors, meant that plan deadlines could not always be met. But perhaps the biggest problem our country faces, which threatens to upset every plan, is its ever-growing population. The fact that we are such a poor country is mainly due to our huge population. We are the second largest country in the world and by the end of this century we shall have about a billion people. India faces the incredibly difficult task of feeding, housing, providing health care and jobs to all these millions of people a task which is almost impossible. In fact, our population problem is so serious that many experts say that only a miracle can save us. Therefore, it is clear, that if our country is to get rid of poverty and to keep progressing, then we must do our utmost to control its population. Therefore, the size of a family must be as small as possible.

India has had to achieve in a very short time what industrialized countries took years to reach. In our hurry to develop industries, modernise the country and cultivate more crops, we have neglected the environment and wasted natural resources, such as water. The huge increase in our population has made the situation worse. In the past, India had more jungles and wildlife. Today, not a single tree can be found in some parts of the country, which were once covered with forests, because we have cut them down for wood, to grow crops or construct houses on that land. Because we have not planted new trees, the climate is changing in many parts of our country. In some areas the land is becoming dry and infertile and in others there is constant flooding. Also, many animals, birds and plant species are dying out. We Indians have never been interested in keeping our surroundings clean, because we do not attach any importance to public hygiene. Our cities are dirty and our rivers full of waste material, but now we are waking up to the seriousness of the problem. Earlier, there were just a handful of groups and individuals who showed some interest in saving the environment. But recently, the government too has taken up the task.

On the whole, in the short time after independence, the Five-Year Plans have helped push the country forward into the modern, industrial age. The main aim behind all these developments is to give, not just a few, but all Indians, a better life. What our country is striving for, is to create a society where there is justice and equality. Also, all Indians should be able to work and earn enough to live decently and have the opportunities to do the things they want to.

So far, we have seen the actual steps taken to remove poverty, inequality and injustice. There is, however, a very important document which contains all that we want our modern Indian state to be. All the steps the government takes are based on this document, which is called

This is our Parliament House - the temple of our democracy. (Overleaf)

Panchayati Raj. At the time of independence our villages were very backward. Gandhiji decided that it was time to bring back an old system— Panchayati Raj. Under this system our villages were to become independent of all outside interventions in internal matters. (Above)

the Constitution. It came into force on January 26, 1950 and was framed under the guidance of Dr. Rajendra Prasad, who later became the first President of our country, and the scheduled caste leader, Dr. B.R. Ambedkar. The Constitution states that everything in India has to be done under the law and that nobody is higher than the Constitution.

According to the Constitution, the country is divided into states and power is shared between the states and the central government. The President is the head of the country and he is assisted by a Vice-President. Parliament, which is the body which makes the laws at the centre, has two houses — the Lok Sabha and the Rajya Sabha. It is the Lok Sabha, which is elected by the people. The Constitution also says that there should be a Cabinet of Ministers led by the Prime Minister, which is to run the country and is responsible to the Lok Sabha. The Constitution also provides for a Supreme Court with a Chief Justice and other judges, and they are the guardians of our Constitution.

At the heart of this document are the pages containing the Fundamental Rights guaranteed to every Indian. The Fundamental Rights, like other parts of the Constitution, have been influenced by Western ideas. These rights include the right to move freely and live wherever one wants and the right to practise the religion one chooses. An important right is the one which guarantees freedom of press and speech. Thus, we have a free press which can criticise government policies without fearing censorship or other forms of interference.

The Fundamental Rights clearly forbid untouchability and discrimination on grounds of religion, race or caste. In fact, our Constitution states that the economic and educational interests of the scheduled castes and tribes should receive special attention. Therefore, people from these groups as well as those belonging to religious minorities are given preferential treatment. For example, seats in the legislatures, universities or jobs are reserved for them, so that they can better their social and economic position. This, as said earlier, is the main issue today.

The Constitution lays down that we are a democratic country with a parliament that is to be elected by the people. This is very important, because it gives all of us, irrespective of class, caste or religion, the right to vote and choose our representatives. The poor peasants in the villages, who form the majority in our country, thus hold a lot of power. Over the years they have become more aware of this. Although most of them are illiterate, they have shown time and again, that they can cast their vote both wisely and cleverly. This has formed the solid base on which Indian democracy rests. Every political party in India knows that if it wants to be elected it has to take into account this huge group of people.

Our Constitution also provides for village panchayats, so that villagers can settle local affairs amongst themselves in a democratic manner. In the past, each caste had its own panchayat. Nowadays members of any caste can be elected to a village panchayat and Harijans and women have seats reserved for them. Although panchayats have brought about a change in village life, they still meet with opposition from the more tradition-bound villagers, still-powerful zamindars, or from money lenders and merchants. The richer members of the higher castes, sometimes use their position in the panchayat, to look after their own interests and not those of the village. Thus, it will take time before the ideal written in our Constitution, becomes a reality.

The territorial waters of India extend into the sea to a distance of twelve nautical miles measured from the appropriate base line.

The boundary of Meghalaya shown on this map is as interpreted from the North-Eastern Areas (Reorganisation) Act, 1971, but has yet to be verified.

The responsibility for correctness of internal details shown on the maps rests with the Publisher.

© Government of India Copyright 1993

Based upon Survey of India map with the permission of the Surveyor General of India.

The administrative headquarters of Haryana and Punjab are at Chandigarh.

India is divided into states and union territories. The system of government in the states is very much like that at the centre. The union territories are, however, administered by the President, acting through an administrator appointed by him. The following are the states and union territories that make up the Union of India.

Andaman and Nicobar Islands

(Union Territory)

Capital	Port Blair
Area	8,293 sq.km
Population	277,989

Andhra Pradesh (State)

Capital	Hyderabad
Area	2,75,068 sq. km.
Population	66,304,854
Languages	Telugu, Urdu

Arunachal Pradesh (State)

Capital	Itanagar
Area	83,743 sq.km
Population	858,392

Assam (State)

Capital	Dispur
Area	78,523 sq.km
Population	22,294,562
Language	Assamese

Bihar (State)

Capital	Patna
Area	1,73,876 sq.km
Population	86,338,853
Language	Hindi

Chandigarh

(Union Territory)

Capital	Chandigarh
Area	114 sq. km.
Population	640,725

Dadra and Nagar Haveli

(Union Territory)

Capital	Silvassa
Area	491 sq.km
Population	138,542

Daman and Diu

(Union Territory)

Capital	Daman
Area	113 sq. km
Population	101,439

Delhi

Capital	Delhi
Area	1,485 sq.km
Population	9,370,475
Languages	Hindi, Punjabi, Urdu

Goa (State)

Capital	Panaji
Area	3,701 sq. km
Population	11,686,22
Languages	Konkani, Marathi, Gujarati

Gujarat (State)

Capital	Gandhinagar
Area	1,95,984 sq.km
Population	41,174,060
Language	Gujarati

Haryana (State)

Capital	Chandigarh
Area	44,212 sq.km
Population	16,317,715
Language	Hindi

Himachal Pradesh (State)

Capital	Shimla
Area	55,673 sq.km
Population	5,111,079
Languages	Hindi, Pahari

Jammu and Kashmir (State)

Capital	Srinagar (Summer) Jammu (Winter)
Area	2,22,236 sq.km
Population	7,718,700
Languages	Kashmiri, Dogri, Urdu, Balti, Gojri, Punjabi, Dardiro, Pahari, Ladakhi

Karnataka (State)

Capital	Bangalore
Area	1,91,791 sq.km
Population	44,817,398
Language	Kannada

Kerala (State)

Capital	Trivandrum
Area	38,864 sq.km
Population	29,011,237
Language	Malayalam

Lakshadweep (Union Territory)

Capital	Kavaratti
Area	32 sq.km
Population	51,681

Madhya Pradesh (State)

Capital	Bhopal
Area	4,42,841 sq.km
Population	66,135,862
Language	Hindi

Maharashtra (State)

Capital	Bombay
Area	3,07,762 sq.,km
Population	78,706,719
Language	Marathi

Manipur (State)

Capital	Imphal
Area	22,356 sq.km
Population	1,826,714
Language	Manipuri

Meghalaya (State)

Capital	Shillong
Area	22,489 sq.km
Population	1,760,626
Languages	Khasi, Prara (Jaintia), Garo

Mizoram (State)

Capital	Aizawl
Area	21,087 sq.km
Population	686,217
Languages	Mizo, English

Nagaland

Capital	Kohima
Area	16,579 sq.km
Population	1,215,573
Language	English

Orissa (State)

Capital	Bhubaneshwar
Area	1,55,782 sq.km.,
Population	31,512,070
Language	Oriya

Pondicherry
(Union Territory)

Capital	Pondicherry
Area	492 sq.km
Population	789,516
Languages	Tamil, French

Punjab (State)

Capital	Chandigarh
Area	50,362 sq.km
Population	20,190,795
Language	Punjabi

Rajasthan (State)

Capital	Jaipur
Area	3,42,239 sq.km
Population	43,880,640
Languages	Rajasthani, Hindi

Sikkim (State)

Capital	Gangtok
Area	7,299 sq.km
Population	403,612
Languages	Bhutia, Nepali, Lepcha, English

Tamil Nadu (State)

Capital	Madras
Area	1,30,069 sq.km.
Population	55,638,318
Language	Tamil

Tripura (State)

Capital	Agartala
Area	10,477 sq.km
Population	2,744,827
Languages	Bengali, Kakborak, Tripuri, Manipuri

Uttar Pradesh (State)

Capital	Lucknow
Area	2,94,413 sq.km
Population	138,760,417
Language	Hindi

West Bengal (State)

Capital	Calcutta
Area	87,853 sq.km
Population	67,982,732
Language	Bengali

Total population of India
843,930,861

Something to be proud of

India is the seventh largest country in the world in terms of area and the second in terms of population. Our country is so huge and diverse that it is known as a subcontinent. This diversity makes India special, as well as different from other countries. Do you remember Mansur, John, Tara and Abong and how different the part of India that each lives in is? The landscape, climate, trees, flowers, animals and birds in Mansur's Kashmir are not the same as those in Tara's Gujarat, John's Kerala, or Abong's Assam. And not only that, the Gods they pray to, the language they speak, the songs they sing and the way they live, are all different. If you were to ask each of them to describe their India, you would have four pictures. So many different images and so many ways of talking about one

country! Well, this is possible, because we Indians can look back to many thousands of years of civilization. This has resulted in a rich cultural past, to which Indians from all parts of the country have contributed. This is our heritage and it is something all of us can be proud of.

Religion

You have probably never thought twice about the fact that in India we have national holidays on all those days which the world's main religions celebrate as their important festivals. It might seem an unimportant fact at first, but when you think about it a little longer, you will realize that this is unique. This is because India is the only country, which has so many religions. Other countries have a main religion, to which the majority of their people belong. Very often in the past, and even now in some countries, other religions were not tolerated. In India, although Hinduism has the largest number of followers, at the time of independence we chose to be a secular country. This means that all religions are given equal importance and this is written into our Constitution. This is nothing new, because our country has had a long tradition of receiving other religions and has, itself given birth to four of the world's religions—Hinduism, Buddhism, Jainism and Sikhism.

Hinduism was founded many thousands of years ago, when the

People offering their prayers in a mosque. (Above)

Krishna—the most popular Hindu God, a favourite of all. (Facing page)

Republic Day sights and exhibits send a shiver of excitement and pride through our spines.

Children awarded for their bravery.

The brave and courageous Indian defence forces. (backleaf)

Aryans came to India. Since then, it has emerged as the religion with the largest number of followers in the country. It has survived the ups and downs of history, and the many reform movements within it, which have resulted in the birth of new religions. It has changed over the ages and absorbed new ideas from other religions. In modern times, the best features of Hinduism could be seen in the person of Mahatma Gandhi, whose exceptional life has taught the world a lot about the Hindu religion. Buddhism and Jainism both emerged from Hinduism about 2,000 years ago, because their founders were dissatisfied with some of the teachings and traditions of Hinduism. While Jainism became an important religion within India, it did not spread outside the country. Buddhism, on the other hand, spread to Sri Lanka, Tibet, South East Asia, China, Japan, Korea and Mongolia. Today, there are more than five million Buddhists and three million Jains in our country.

The last of the four religions, which have their roots in our country is Sikhism. It is also the youngest of India's various religions, having been founded in 1500 A.D. by Guru Nanak. Sikhism started as a reform movement, as it rejected the teachings of both Hinduism and Islam. There are more than 14 million Sikhs living in India and there are many who have migrated to other parts of the world.

Islam is not a religion which had its origins in India, but it has had a tremendous influence on our country. So great has been its impact that Muslims are the second largest group in India today, with over 100 million followers. This also makes India the country with the second largest Muslim population in the world.

There are two more important religious groups in our country—the Parsis and the Christians. The Zoroastrians or Parsis fled from Iran and sought refuge in India as long back as the seventh century A.D. Today, they are a small, but wealthy group. The first Christians came to our country soon after the death of Christ. But, it is in the last hundred years that Christianity has influenced the thinking of Hindus. Men like Rammohun Roy and Mahatma Gandhi were deeply influenced by Christian ideas and thoughts and they tried to bring some of these into Hinduism.

Language and Literature

Nowhere in the world do the people of the same country speak so many different languages as in India. Foreigners very often think that all Indians speak one language called 'Indian' and sometimes they even think that all of us speak English! "How ignorant," you would say. When foreigners are told that India has 14 official languages and thousands of different dialects they find it unbelievable that all of us belong to one country and yet do not share such an important thing as a common language. A Frenchman can make himself understood all over France. If he decides to spend a holiday in England, he may have

The Golden Temple in Amritsar, is held in high regard by Sikhs as the holiest of shrines. (Facing page)

trouble speaking English, but he can at least try to read English because the two languages share the same script. But what about a Gujarati who decides to visit Tamil Nadu? Most probably, he will be at a loss, because neither can he speak Tamil, nor can he guess what is written, as the Tamil script is totally different from Gujarati. Of course, this makes things quite difficult in our country, not only as far as governing it is concerned, but also because ideas and thoughts cannot flow so easily from one place to another. But, at the same time, this unique feature of our country is something to be proud of, because each one of our languages has a rich history behind it and each is a part of our cultural heritage.

The earliest known language in India came with the Aryans, thousands of years ago. This was known as Vedic or the language of the Vedas and it later developed into Sanskrit. The oldest Aryan text that has survived is a collection of hymns to the Gods, called *Rigveda-sanhita*, which is more than 3,000 years old. Amongst the most famous works in Sanskrit were the *Mahabharata* — the longest poem in the world — and the *Ramayana*. But the greatest Sanskrit poet and writer was Kalidasa who lived in the fifth century A.D. All of us know about his poem *Meghdoot* and his play *Shakuntala*. Over the years, Sanskrit ceased to be the everyday language, but was used only by learned men and writers. And then came a time when even scholars stopped

speaking and writing in Sanskrit, but still it never completely died out. In fact, even today, we learn Sanskrit in our schools and those of us who are really interested can continue studying it at the university.

Hindi, in one form or another, is the language spoken by most people in the northern Indian states. Since it is also generally understood by the largest number of people in India, it was chosen to be our national language after independence. So, all of us learn some level of Hindi in school. Hindi literature's most famous name was the poet Tulsidas, who lived in the 16th century A.D. His *Ramacharitamanas* is, till today, one of the most important books of our country. It was in the 19th century that Hindi literature began to change and adjust itself to the times. The person who brought in this change was 'Bharatendu' Harishchandra. But the man, who with his novels and short-stories, set the foundation for modern Hindi literature and drew attention to it, was the 20th century writer Premchand.

Urdu is the language spoken by millions of Muslims and very many Hindus in various parts of India, such as Uttar Pradesh, Bihar and Andhra Pradesh. It was the language used in the royal courts of Golconda and Bijapur in south India and later, Lucknow and Hyderabad. From the 16th to the 19th century, Urdu literature flourished in these places. We have all heard of Ghalib, the famous Urdu poet of the early 19th century. As the struggle with the British began, Urdu writers became the voice of the nationalists in the country. Also, they began to pay attention to the social and political problems faced by the Muslims at this time. After independence, the Urdu language has continued to produce poets, novelists and short-story writers. Amongst them is Qurratulain Haider, who was born in 1928. She has written excellent novels about the Muslim upper class and the changes that have taken place in their lives in recent years.

Noteworthy in Indian literature is the Kashmiri poetry of the 14th century, and in Punjabi, the beautiful poetry of Guru Nanak written in the 15th century.

Literature has a long tradition in Bengal, Orissa and Assam and it dates back to many centuries. In the 19th and 20th centuries, Bengal produced many great writers. Amongst them were Ishwarchandra Vidyasagar, who wrote about social problems and Saratchandra Chatterjee, whose novels are read all over India. Bankim Chandra Chatterjee and Michael Madhusudan Datta, were also equally well-known. But the greatest among them and probably the most important modern Indian writer was Rabindranath Tagore, who was born in 1861 and died in 1941. He was a genius, who in his lifetime, wrote many poems, novels and short-stories, as well as songs and dance-dramas, and towards the end of his life, even turned to painting. He also founded the Vishwa Bharati university at Santiniketan. Rabindranath Tagore is also the only Indian who has won the Nobel Prize

for literature.

The earliest Marathi as well as Gujarati literature goes back to the 13th and 14th centuries. Most of these early works were religious poems. In the 19th and 20th centuries, novels, short-stories and plays were also written. Govardhanram Tripathi's *Saraswatchandra*, written in the beginning of the 20th century, is considered to be the greatest Gujarati novel. Mahatma Gandhi also wrote a lot in his mother tongue, Gujarati. Today, the works of the Gujarati poet Umashankar Joshi, are known all over India. In Maharashtra, in the beginning of the 20th century, men like Lokmanya Tilak and N.C. Kelkar wrote in a language that was powerful and passionate. But Marathi literature is most well-known through its plays. There were the great playwrights Deval, Khadilkar, Gadkari and Kolhatkar and today, Vijay Tendulkar's plays are performed all over India.

Tamil, Telugu, Kannada and Malayalam have a very rich literature with a long tradition behind them. In fact, of all the languages of India, Tamil literature can trace its history from its beginnings in the second century A.D., till today, without any gaps, and this makes it older than any other literature in the country. The earliest collection of poems in Tamil known as *Sangam literature*, was so developed that it has no parallels even in Sanskrit. Telugu literature can be traced to the 11th century, while Kannada literature had its origins in the 9th century. Most of the early literature in all these languages was poetry. As the literature of the other languages in our country changed with the coming of the British it also did in South India. Novels, short stories, essays and plays began to be written in the 19th and 20th centuries. Subramaniam Bharati and V V S. Aiyar were leading Tamil writers in the 19th century. Rao Bahadur K. Viresalingam Pantalu was the first modern Telugu writer. And in Malayalam, there were three great poets early this century—Kumaran Asan, Valluthol Narayana Menon and Ulloor Parameswara Iyer.

Despite our regional languages and literary traditions, many Indians have written in English. Rabindranath Tagore won the Nobel Prize for literature in 1913, for the English translation of Gitanjali, a collection of poems he wrote in Bengali. Another person of great importance was Dr. Sarvepalli Radhakrishnan, whose writings in English did much to make not only us Indians, but also foreigners, aware of Hindu religion and philosophy. In recent times, lots of Indians living in India and abroad have written novels, short stories and poetry in English. Amongst them are Nirad C. Chaudhuri and R K Narayan. The younger generation of writers in English include Nissim Ezekiel, A K. Ramanujan, Anita Desai and Salman Rushdie.

Science

Science in our country has a long tradition behind it. Mathematics,

Rabindranath Tagore — a great thinker, philosopher and writer, he was awarded the Nobel Prize for Literature in 1913. (Facing page)

Rakesh Sharma —India's
first man in space.

astronomy, medicine — all these subjects have their roots in the period when the Aryans came and settled down in India. In course of time, Indians developed the system of numbers on which all science is based. This knowledge passed from India, through the Arab countries, to Europe. It was probably one of our country's biggest gifts to the world. India, through the ages, developed and perfected the art of weaving and each region produced a different kind of cloth. Our country, for a long time, was the largest exporter of textiles in the world, until the British came. Not only that, the manufacture of pottery, glass and the production of iron and steel were carried on in India, and was of a high quality. In fact, it was only sometime in the 18th century, that India, although still one of the world's leading industrial nations, began to fall behind in the development of new technologies.

In the early years of British rule, the development of science and technology came to a standstill. However, despite difficulties, the situation began to improve, thanks to changes gradually brought about in the educational system by the British, and later on through our own efforts. A new generation of scientists emerged. Amongst them were the biochemist J C Bose, physicists C V Raman, Krishnan and S N Bose, astrophysicist M N Saha and mathematician S. Ramanujan. They all did

An artist's conception of INSAT space craft in the geostationary orbit. (Below)

important work in the early 20th century and C V Raman was awarded the Nobel Prize for physics in 1930.

After independence, India had to achieve a lot within a very short time. Three scientists who set up important government research centres were, the chemist S S Bhatnagar who organized the Council of Scientific and Industrial Research; physicist H J Bhabha, who headed the Tata Institute of Fundamental Research and then set up the Department of Atomic Energy, and physicist V Sarabhai, who built up the govenment's Department of Space. India has built nuclear reactors, launched satellites and now stepped into the computer age. Today, science is one of the most popular subjects in our schools. We have the third largest system of higher education in the world and it includes excellent institutions like the Indian Institutes of Technology, the Indian Institute of Science and the research centres of the Council of Scientific and Industrial Research. These have enabled Indians to contribute to modern science. Unfortunately, many talented scientists today, choose to go abroad after completing their basic studies at home. Quite a few of them occupy important positions in universities and research centres in Europe and the United States. For example, H G Khorana in medicine and S Chandrasekhar in physics, have won the Nobel Prize for work they did in the U S as American citizens.

Architecture

Many of you may be fortunate to find old temples or mosques or even old fortresses close to the place where you live. I say fortunate, because not many people are lucky to live near beautiful monuments, leave alone many kinds of them. Take Delhi for example, with its famous Qutab Minar, its many fortresses and the impressive Raj Path and Rashtrapati Bhavan. But not many people in Delhi or elsewhere, realize that the architectural beauty they are surrounded by is what people in many other countries do not have and can only dream of.

But what do we have? To begin with, our ancestors have handed down to us the first urban settlements in the world at Mohenjodaro and Harappa. Today, only ruins remain, but from them we can reconstruct what the settlements looked like nearly 5,000 years ago. Our country is also known for its religious architecture. There are Buddhist stupas, built by Ashoka in the third century B.C., as well as exquisite Jain temples at Mount Abu. Hindu temples are famous for their combination of sculpture and architecture, like the temples at Khajuraho and Bhubaneshwar and the huge Madurai temple in the south. There are beautiful Hindu palaces like the one in Vijayanagar in south India. Muslims introduced a new architectural style into the sub-continent. The rich architectural heritage of this period includes the mosques at Delhi, Fatehpur Sikri and Agra. Both Hindus and Muslims built impressive fortresses like the Hindu forts in Rajasthan and the Muslim ones at

The Gwalior Fort — the ancient hill fort of Gwalior. Man Singh's palace and Hathiapaur, Elephant Gate. (Facing page)

Bhuwaneshwar Temple —
Temple of Lingaraja sits in
the centre of a large
quadrangular precinct,
surrounded by a high wall
and a trench.

The Shore Temple —
rock temples of
Mahabalipuram. Built in the
late seventh and early
eighth century A.D. It was
constructed out of cut stone
blocks. It was built by
Narsimha Varman II,
Rajasimha and is dedicated
to Lord Shiva.

The city palace at Jaipur was built in early eighteenth century. The variety of different arch-shapes picked out on the pink painted walls are characteristic of late Rajput decorations. (Left)

Ahmedabad and Bijapur. The Mughuls also built beautiful tombs, the most famous being the Taj Mahal built by the emperor Shah Jahan. With the arrival of the Europeans, another kind of architecture was brought into the country. Apart from the Portuguese churches in Goa, there are the Viceroy's residences, churches and university buildings built by the British, who also drew up the original plans for New Delhi. After independence, Chandigarh was designed by the French architect Le Corbusier. Nowadays, most buildings all over the country show the influence of Western architecture.

A haveli in Jaisalmer —the elaborate stone screens serve a purpose since Purdah is still observed here. (Below)

Sixty miles north-east of Aurangabad, Western India, over the winding bed of Waghora river extends a rocky hill, some 260 feet high. Some thirty caves are cut out of its sides along a stretch of forty yards. Five of them, *chaitya* - halls and rest monasteries, they are world famous today for their magnificent paintings. This is a detail from an Ajanta painting dated to the last quarter of the fifth century.

Shah Jahan "A good portrait of mine in my twenty fifth year", so read the inscription on the margin of this painting by Abul Hasan, 1617. In his hand, Shah Jahan is holding a turban jewel.

Painting and Sculpture

Unfortunately, not much of ancient Indian painting has survived to the present day. In early times, the walls of houses, palaces and temples must have been covered with paintings, all of which are now lost. One can only guess the value of that which has disappeared when one sees the beautiful wall-paintings in the caves at Ajanta, which were painted between the second century B.C. and the fifth century A.D. Most early Hindu, Buddhist and Jain paintings were done on the walls of caves, and some have survived in Karnataka, Tamil Nadu and Maharashtra. Many Buddhist and Jain religious drawings between the 11th and 14th centuries A.D., were done on palm-leaf pages or cloth. However, it was the Muslims who introduced paper into the country and along with it, the art of illustrating books. Under the Mughuls, book-painting and miniature painting reached a high degree of perfection. Miniature painting was adapted to local traditions in Rajasthan and the hill areas,

This painting depicts mortal lovers,Radha and Krishna,turn divine. They are seated on a gigantic Lotus flower. Also placed on the flower is a cascade. The poet –prince, Krishna, opens it in order to raise the *paan* to *bani-thani* Radha's lips. (Below)

This is a 5 AD terracotta of the river Goddess, Ganga, from the temple of Ahichhatra in Uttar Pradesh.

such as Kangra and Garhwal. All of them soon became important centres of this form of painting. The British brought European art into the country, the influence of which still continues. In this century, painters like Abanindranath Tagore, Nandalal Bose, Abdur Rehman Chaghatai and later, Jamini Roy tried to create a new Indian style. Artists like Amrita Shergil, Ravi Verma and Satish Gujral, however, tried to paint Indian themes combining Western and Indian styles. The younger generation of artists includes Bhupen Khakhar, Sudhir Patwardhan and Gulammohamed Sheikh.

Sculpture has always played an important role in Indian art and was mostly used to decorate temples. Though some sculpture from the Indus Valley civilization had been found, some of the most beautiful pieces were those done during the time of the Mauryas in the third century B.C. and the Guptas in the fourth century A.D. In the south, there are the famous sculptures of Mahabalipuram in Tamil Nadu. In Karnataka, there are also excellent sculptures made between the sixth and 12th centuries A.D. While in north India sculpture was mostly in stone, some of south India's most famous works were done in bronze. The old Indian tradition of sculpture is still alive, and modern works by sculptors like Ram Kinkar and Debi Prasad Raychaudhuri, are displayed in our big cities.

The famous figure of Shiva as Natraj — the Lord of Dance. In his right hand is damru, the symbol of creation and in his left is the fire of destruction.

A 16 century copper statue of Pootna and Krishna. Karnataka. (Below)

Music

    As with the other fine arts, our country's musical tradition stretches back over centuries and has come down to us in very much the same form as it existed in the past. Our music has been passed orally from one generation to another. You probably know that there are two distinct styles of Indian classical music—Hindustani music of the north and Karnatak music of the south. Amir Khusrau in the 13th century and later Tansen, one of Akbar's 'nine jewels', are two of the famous names in Hindustani music. Karnatak music owes much to three composers—Tyagaraja, Svami Shastri and Dikshitar—all three of whom lived in the 18th century. Classical instrumental music is still very popular and part of it is due to the personality of today's musicians and the diversity of instruments they perform on. Ravi Shankar on the sitar, Alla Rakha and Zakir Hussain on the tabla, Bismillah Khan's shehnai, Hari Prasad Chaurasia on the flute, Amjad Ali Khan on the sarod and Shiv Kumar Sharma on the santoor, are all names we have heard of. Classical vocal music has been just as popular and artistes like Bhimsen Joshi, Kishoribai Amonkar, Mallikarjun Mansoor and Kumar Gandharva have brought pleasure to millions.

    Of course, we also have a rich variety of folk and religious music. Every region of India has its own folk songs, which are sung at

Pandit Bhim Sen Joshi —a leading exponent of Indian classical vocal music. (Above)

Pandit Ravi Shankar — the unparalleled Sitar Maestro. (Facing page)

harvesting time, during festivals or while working. Religious music includes Hindu *bhajans* and Muslim *quavvalis*. Finally, we must mention Indian film music. It may not be as sophisticated as classical music or as close to the soil as folk music, but it has become a part of modern Indian life and is extremely popular, no matter which part of the country one is in. Can you imagine a day without hearing film songs sung by Lata Mangeshkar, Mohammed Rafi or Kishore Kumar, somewhere on the radio or television?

Dance

It seems that we Indians have been dancing for as long a time as we have been playing music or singing songs, or perhaps even longer! The story of Indian dance goes back to 2500 B.C., to the Indus Valley Civilization. Dance was from the very beginning associated with religion and the worship of the Gods. Till today, our classical dances — Bharata Natyam, Odissi, Manipuri, Kathak, Kathakali and Kuchipudi are all based on religious themes. Bharata Natyam, mainly a solo dance, still has its centre in Tamil Nadu, while Kathakali, which comes from Kerala, has a number of dancers playing the role of different characters

Zubin Mehta —conducting a Western classical orchestra. (Right)

From the desert regions of Rajasthan comes the colourfully tuned Langas. Their rich-voiced renditions of love and heroic ballads are accompanied by Sarangi, wood claps and drums. (Below)

Dhrupad is the oldest
music-form in Indian
classical music.

A Rajasthani musician
with a traditional
instrument. (Left)

in a dance-drama. Kuchipudi, from Andhra Pradesh, is also a dance-drama form, which has many similarities with Bharata Natyam. Odissi, is a solo dance form from Orissa and was originally performed in the temple. Kathak, on the other hand, is a northern Indian dance form which was associated with the Muslim courts in Lucknow. Manipuri dance comes from the eastern part of India and is quite different from Bharata Natyam and Odissi. Dancers like Thankamani, Balasaraswathi, Ram Gopal and Uday Shankar brought about a revival of interest in Indian classical dance. Some of the leading dancers of the past few years have been Yamini Krishnamurthi and Indrani Rehman (Bharata Natyam), Sonal Mansingh (Odissi) and Raja and Radha Reddy (Kuchipudi).

Folk dance, like folk music is performed on occasions like festivals or during harvesting. Each part of India has its own special folk dance. We have all seen, or perhaps even participated in Gujarat's Garba dance, the Punjabi Bhangra, Tamil Nadu's Pinnal Kolattam or the Assamese Bihu.

Cinema

When Dadasheb Phalke made his first film in 1913, he introduced us

Birju Maharaj — a foremost exponent of Kathak—a dance form based on complex rhythms. It involves clapping, stamping and bell ringing in dialogue with an ensemble of percussionists.

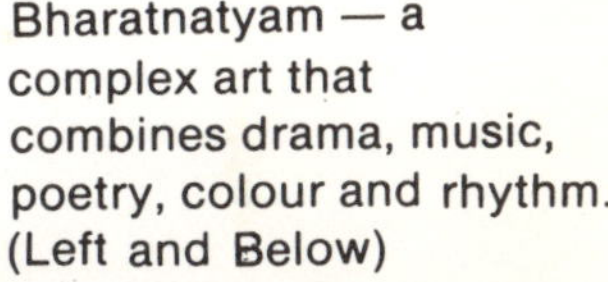

Bharatnatyam — a complex art that combines drama, music, poetry, colour and rhythm. (Left and Below)

Gurudutt in *Kagaz Ke Phool.*

Raj Kapoor and Nargis in *Shree 420.* (Right)

to a form of entertainment which is the most popular in India today. It has been a long journey from the early days of the silent film to today's big, glossy Indian movies. The development of films in India took place at almost the same time as in Europe and USA. But it has taken such firm roots in our country that we produce more films than in Europe and we are now USA's biggest competitors. Hundreds of Hindi films are made in Bombay every year and in Tamil, Telugu and other regional languages all over India. Indian films are exported to Egypt, Africa and

Meena Kumari & Rehman in *Sahab, Bibi Aur Ghulam*.

Gurudutt, Shakila & Johnny Walker in *Aar Paar*.

the Far East and to USA and many European countries.

Although the most popular movies are those with big stars, songs and dances and lots of action, they are not the ones that have made Indian movies well-known all over the world. Men like Shantaram, Bimal Roy, Guru Dutt and Raj Kapoor, made Hindi films which till today are unbeaten in quality. And it was the talent of actors and actresses like Sohrab Modi, Prithviraj Kapoor, Devika Rani, Ashok Kumar, Durga Khote, Kananbala Devi, Dilip Kumar, Nargis and Meena Kumari, which made many films unforgettable. But the man who made Indian cinema known all over the world and showed that film-making was an art in India, was the film-director Satyajit Ray. He was followed by many others, such as Mrinal Sen, Ritwik Ghatak, Shyam Benegal and Adoor Gopalakrishnan. They, along with actors and actresses like Shabana Azmi, Naseeruddin Shah, Om Puri and Smita Patil have kept up the tradition of India's art films.

Radio and Television

Although radio and television are not as popular as cinema, nor are the programmes as sophisticated or well-made, they deserve to be mentioned. In a huge country like ours, they play an important role, although we have not been able to use this media to the fullest extent.

The most striking feature of the electronic media—radio and television—in our country is that, unlike newspapers, they are controlled by the government. This has resulted in the government often using both All India Radio and Doordarshan for its own purposes. It was suggested as far back as 1966 that an independent broadcasting corporation be set up. However, no action was taken till 1989, when the matter was introduced in Parliament. However, this Bill has yet to be finalized.

While radio has spread almost throughout the country and plays an important role in the rural areas, television is less widespread and has a strong urban character. This can be seen in the kind of advertisements that are shown on television. Most of the products advertised are for city and town dwellers, and that too, the richer sections of society.

In recent years, our television programmes have changed considerably. Nowadays a lot of soap operas appear on television, and these have become strong competitors of the Hindi film.

Sport

There are many sports and games which have been played in our country for a long time. Chess, which originated in India in the sixth century A.D. is probably the best known traditional game. Card games and dice-playing are also old Indian pastimes. Other typically Indian sports, particularly in the rural areas, are wrestling and kabaddi. Hunting and polo also have a long tradition behind them, though it was the upper classes or the nobility which participated in these sports.

Pitampura TV Tower. Sending out the message of development to every home in India. (Facing page)

Vijay Amritraj, the foremost Indian lawn-tennis player. He has captained the Indian team at many international tennis tournaments. (Overleaf).

Today two types of sports are very popular in India—cricket and hockey. Ever since Prince Ranjitsinhji popularized cricket in India, there has been no shortage of talented players. The Indian hockey team dominated the sport for many years and you must have heard about the hockey wizard Dhyanchand. But recent changes in playing conditions have resulted in the Indians having to give way to the Europeans and Australians. Other games like football, volleyball, badminton and tennis are also played in the country. The last two have produced individual players of world repute like Prakash Padukone (badminton) and Ramanathan Krishnan and Vijay Amritraj (tennis). Mountaineering is also gaining in popularity. And in this most rugged and demanding of sports, one name deserves to be mentioned, that of Bacchendri Pal. She is the first Indian woman (and the fifth in the world) to have climbed Mount Everest. Bacchendri Pal has done a lot to make mountaineering popular in India and to improve conditions for mountaineers in the country.

Sunil Gavaskar, the hero of Indian Cricket. He holds many records for achievement in Cricket. Recognized internationally, 'Sunny' is an inspiration to every young cricketer. His classic style of batting has been very much appreciated by cricket-pundits. Kapil Dev, a wonderful all-round cricketer, he helped India win her first World Cricket Cup in 1983. His fast pace bowling and his unconventional sixers have always won him admirers. (Above)

Conclusion

Our country's enormous size, huge population and abundant resources make it difficult for other nations to ignore us. Besides, geographically, we are located in such a position on the map that we are bound to become the meeting place of not only different parts of Asia, but of the East and West. Thus, our country has played and continues to play, an important role in world affairs both culturally and politically. India has at times been pushed to the forefront by the peculiar situation prevailing in the world. This happened particularly after the second World War when, due to the different ways in which the Americans and the Russians thought that society should function and be governed, the world was sharply divided into two blocs, led by these two powers. Nehru decided that India should follow an independent policy and not belong to either side. In the process he linked India to other developing Asian and African countries who followed the same policy which came to be termed non-alignment.

Today they realise that they have much in common and that they can jointly solve many of their problems.

We just referred to India's important geographical position in Asia. This, together with the fact that Indian culture once flourished in southeast Asia and that India also had contacts with western and central Asia, has impelled modern India to revive these old ties. Special efforts have been made to further trade, economic interests and cultural ties with our immediate neighbours—Pakistan, Bangladesh, Nepal, Sri Lanka, Bhutan and China. As India endeavours to strengthen its Asian roots, it becomes a more pressing duty for all of us who live in this great sprawling country to preserve our inner strength as a peaceful, civilized, and democratic nation. Many diverse languages, cultures and religions have merged to make us a distinct entity, unique in the world today. It is up to us to maintain this special feature of our country.

Some Indians This Century

Rukmini Devi Arundale (1904-1986)

Born in the temple town of Madurai, Rukmini Devi Arundale came under the influence of Annie Besant and George Arundale, two theosophists who were not only well-known for their selfless service but also for their unconventional approach to life. She shocked the conservative Indian society of that time by marrying George Arundale, an Australian, and took to dancing which till then was associated with temple dancers. It was she who gave the name *Bharata Natyam* to the dance form traditionally known as *Chinna Melam*. Meenakshisundaram Pillai was her guru and she gave her first dance recital in 1935.

Rukmini Devi Arundale founded the International Art Centre at Kalakshetra, Madras in 1936. In 1957, she was made a Fellow of the Sangeet Natak Akademi. She was given the title 'Deshikotama' by Vishwa Bharati University and was awarded the Padma Bhushan in 1956. Rukmini Devi Arundale was also a member of the Rajya Sabha.

Shabana Azmi (Born 1955)

Shabana Azmi has been acting in films for nearly twenty years now, and has achieved success as an actress in both art as well as commercial cinema. She won the Government of India's National Award for Best Actress in 1975 *(Ankur)*, 1981 *(Arth)*, 1982 *(Khandar)* and 1984 *(Paar)*.

Over the years, people have also come to know Shabana Azmi as a feminist concerned with the rights of women in Indian society. Her views are reflected in the roles she plays, where she often portrays the intelligent and independent woman.

Kamaladevi Chattopadhyay (1903-1988)

Kamaladevi Chattopadhyay was a many-faceted person. As a young woman she was influenced by Mahatma Gandhi and left her comfortable home to take part in the national struggle for independence. She joined the Indian National Congress and was elected to the All India Congress Committee in 1927. During this time she spent five years in jail.

Kamaladevi Chattopadhyay did her

Rukmini Devi Arundale

Shabana Azmi

Kamaladevi Chattopadhyay

utmost to help in the task of nation-building. She founded the Indian Cooperative Union in 1948 to help rehabilitate refugees. It was largely due to her efforts that thousands of refugees from Pakistan were resettled in Faridabad, Haryana. Kamaladevi Chattopadhyay is remembered for reviving interest in our country's handicrafts. She was also interested in women's issues and was the organizing secretary and President of the All India Women's Conference.

In 1970, she was awarded the title 'Deshikotama' by Vishwa Bharati University. A recipient of the UNESCO Award in 1977, she was also honoured with the Magsaysay Award.

M.S. Subbulakshmi (born 1906)

The singer of Karnatik music, M S Subbulakshmi, is one of our country's most famous classical singers. She began her career at a very young age when she performed along with her mother. Soon she was giving solo recitals in India and abroad.

M S Subbulakshmi has supported social and religious causes by giving benefit performances and donating the royalties from many of her records. She was given the Magsaysay Award for Public Service in

recognition of her social work. She is also the recipient of numerous other awards and titles, including the Padma Vibhushan (1975).

Prasanta Chandra Mahalanobis (1893-1972)

P C Mahalanobis was educated in Calcutta and at Cambridge University. He returned from Cambridge to become Professor of Physics at Presidency College, Calcutta from 1922 and was its Principal from 1945 to 48. Best known for his role in planning and development, P.C. Mahalanobis was made Member, Planning Commission in 1955.

P C Mahalanobis was, from 1931, Secretary and later Director of the Indian Statistical Institute. In 1954, he was Chairman of the United Nations Statistical Commission. A Fellow of the Indian Academy of Sciences, he was also a Member of the USSR Academy of Sciences and a Fellow of the Royal Society (England). P C Mahalanobis was awarded the Padma Vibhushan in 1968.

Indira Gandhi (1917-1984)

Indira Gandhi was India's third Prime Minister and one of the few women to be the head of the government. The only child

M.S. Subbulakshmi

Prasanta Chandra Mahalanobis

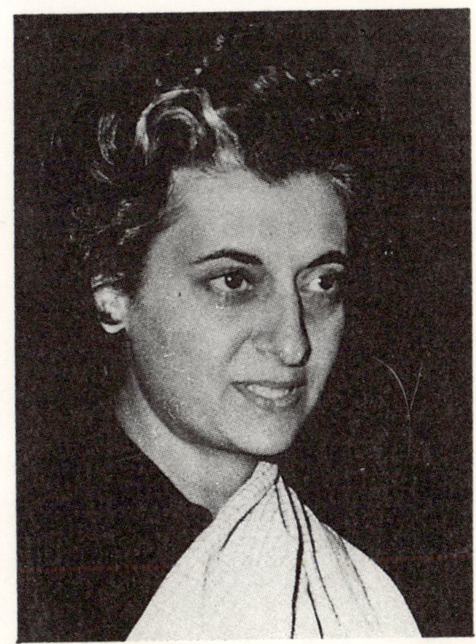

Indira Gandhi

of Jawaharlal Nehru, Indira Gandhi grew up with politics and thus learnt much about it from her father.

In her younger days these lessons were in the form of letters which he wrote to her from prison. Later on, when he became Prime Minister, she learnt through helping her father as his political aide and hostess. This experience was useful for her own political career as a member of the Congress Party, as a minister, and later on as Prime Minister. Indira Gandhi's years as Prime Minister from 1966 to 1977 and from 1980 to 1984 were marked by a determined leadership which she showed, for example, during the war to liberate Bangladesh. With her progressive attitude she tried to bring about change not only within the Congress Party, but in the country as well. Amongst the many honours she received was the nation's highest honour, the Bharat Ratna.

Sunil Manohar Gavaskar (born 1949)

Sunil Manohar Gavaskar was born into a family which took a keen interest in cricket. Therefore, it is not surprising that he started playing cricket at a very young age. He distinguished himself at school and university level cricket before playing at the national level in the Ranji Trophy matches.

In 1971, Gavaskar made his test debut at Port of Spain, Trinidad. He played for the Rest of the World in Australia in 1971 to 72. Sunil Gavaskar represented India and was captain of its national team in 32 test matches between 1978 and 1983. He hit 34 centuries in test cricket, and his score of 236 against West Indies in 1983 is the highest by any Indian in test cricket Sunil Gavaskar won the Arjuna Award in 1975 and was honoured with the Padma Bhushan in 1980.

Maqbool Fida Husain (born 1915)

The painter M F Husain was born in Sholapur, Maharashtra. In 1948 he joined the Progressive Artists Group and two years later he held his first exhibition in Bombay. Since then his paintings have been shown in places as diverse as London, Prague, Tokyo, New York and Baghdad. Amongst his major works are the murals for the WHO building in Delhi and for the Aligarh University The artist Husain made a well-known award winning film called "Through the Eyes of a Painter" He has been a member of the Lalit Kala Akademi and sat in the Rajya Sabha as a nominated member of Parliament.

Sunil Manohar Gavaskar

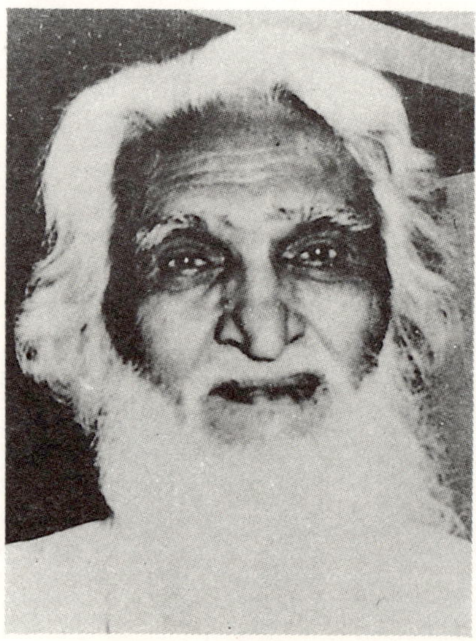

Maqbool Fida Husain

Tenzing Norgay

Tenzing Norgay (1914-1986)

In 1953 Tenzing Norgay stood at the top of the world when he and Edmund Hillary became the first men to climb Mount Everest. He was born in Nepal, close to the mountains, and as a child loved to listen to stories of mountain climbing. In 1932 he migrated to Bengal. Young Tenzing Norgay participated as a porter in various Himalayan expeditions before joining the one in 1953 that was to make him famous. He received many honours and awards as a result of this feat. Amongst them were the Star of Nepal (1953), the British Coronation Medal (1953) and the Hubbard Medal of the American National Geographic Society. In 1954, the Indian government made him the first Director of the Himalayan Mountaineering Institute in Darjeeling.

R.K. Narayan (born 1906)

Novelist and short story writer, R K Narayan was born in Madras. At the age of two he was sent by his parents to live with his grandmother and uncle. In an interview he once said that during his early school days he was rather alone and his best friends were a peacock and a monkey.

Very early he realised that what he wanted to do most was to write. With his first novel 'Swami and Friends' began a long series of novels and short stories which have made him one of the world's best writers. His most famous creation is *Malgudi*, an imaginary town which is typically Indian.

Sarvepalli Radhakrishnan (1888-1975)

Intellectual, philosopher and writer, S. Radhakrishnan was educated at Madras Christian College. During his illustrious academic career, he was professor at the Universities of Mysore, Calcutta and later Oxford. He became Vice-Chancellor of the Banaras Hindu University in 1942.

After India's independence in 1947, he was made Chairman, University Education Commission. S. Radhakrishnan was also our country's chief delegate to UNESCO, whose Chairman he became in 1952. Amongst the political posts he held were member of the Rajya Sabha and, of course, he was Vice-President 1952-56 and 1957-62 and subsequently, President of our country from 1962 to 66.

V.K.R.V. Rao (1908-1991)

The economist V.K.R.V. Rao was educated at Bombay University and Cambridge

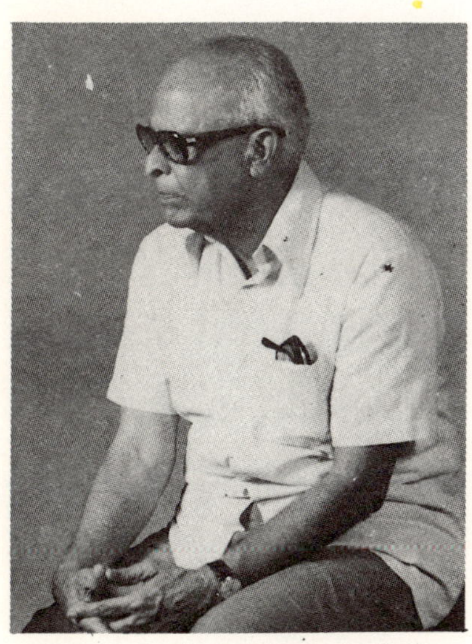

R.K. Narayan

Sarvepalli Radhakrishnan

V.K.R.V. Rao

University. After teaching at Ahmedabad, he was Professor and Head of the Department of Economics, Delhi University from 1942 to 57. He founded the well-known Delhi School of Economics and was its Director from 1949 to 57. V.K.R.V. Rao was Vice-Chancellor of Delhi University in 1957 to 60. Between 1960 and 1961 he set up the Institute of Economic Growth.

V.K.R.V. Rao was a member of various Committees and Commissions of the Indian Government. He was Planning Adviser to the Government from 1945 to 46 and in 1963 was appointed a member of the Planning Commission. V.K.R.V. Rao also held several ministerial posts and was a member of parliament. He was awarded the Padma Vibhushan in 1974.

Satyajit Ray (1922-1992)

As a young man Satyajit Ray wanted to become a scientist. But due to the influence of Rabindranath Tagore, who was a friend of his family, he started studying art. Although he never lost his interest in art, his mind turned to film-making. With money collected from different sources he made his first film *Pather Panchali* in 1955. This was the first of a series of three films which were to earn him a place amongst the worlds best film makers. Satayajit Ray won prizes at all the prestigious film festivals including an Oscar for his contribution to world cinema. Most of his films are beautiful and poetic with a tremendous eye for detail.

Kunwar Sain (born 1899)

Kunwar Sain was born in Tohana village in Punjab where only a vernacular school existed. But the brilliant student was not to be checked. A series of unusual events led him to Roorkee Engineering College, from where he graduated in 1922. It is to Kunwar Sain that we owe many of our irrigation projects such as the Hirakud in Orissa, Kosi in Nepal and the massive Bhakra Nangal dam in Punjab.

He was honoured with the Padma Bhushan.

Monkombu S Swaminathan (born 1925)

After independence, the country's first task was to develop its agricultural capacity. The man behind the 'Green Revolution' which resulted in India's self-sufficiency in feeding its own people, was M S Swaminathan. He was educated in Madras and at the

Satyajit Ray

Kunwar Sain

Monkombu Sambasivan Swaminathan

University of Cambridge and has held important positions in India and abroad. He was Director General, Indian Council for Agricultural Research (1972-79), a member of the Planning Commission (1980-82), Director General International Rice Research Institute (Philippines) and   Chairman UN Advisory Committee on Science and Technology.

M.S. Swaminathan has won numerous awards He is a Fellow of the Indian Academy of Sciences, and is a member of prestigious British, United States and Russian scientific organizations.

Devidas Murlidar Amte (born 1914)

Devidas Murlidar Amte or Baba Amte as he is known, received an education in law. But it is for his involvement in social work that he is best known. He established the huge leper colony near Nagpur. For his social engagement, Baba Amte has been given several honours including the Padma Shree (1971), Magsaysay Award (1985), the Padma Vibhushan (1986), the UN Human Rights Award, and the Templeton Prize for Progress in Religion.

Apart from his work for lepers, Baba Amte has led six peace missions to the disturbed state of Punjab between 1985 and 1987. He has also raised his voice against environmental disasters in India, such as his recent opposition to the proposed plan to construct a dam on the Narmada river.

Sunderlal Bahuguna (born 1927)

Born in the Himalayan region, Sunderlal Bahuguna began as a teacher before he became interested in social work. He set up a hostel for children in the Garhwal area. Influenced by the Sarvodaya movement he founded an ashram at Silyara in Garhwal.

Sunderlal Bahuguna is well-known for having started the "Chipko" movement in the seventies. He saw the disastrous effect that mass-scale deforestation was having on the lives of the people, especially the women, of the region. Through the "Chipko" movement the local population and indeed people all over India became aware of the critical state of the environment in the Himalayas. Sunderlal Bahuguna walked about 15,000 km through his beloved Himalayas spreading his ideas about conservation.

Mother Teresa (born 1906)

Most of us have heard of Mother Teresa or

Devidas Murlidar Amte

Sunderlal Bahuguna

Mother Teresa

seen photographs of the small stooped woman—probably India's most well-known missionary. Though she is now an Indian citizen, she was born in Albania and left home at the age of fifteen to work as a missionary in Bengal. She began by teaching, and was Principal, St. Mary's High School, Calcutta, but the terrible poverty around her made her decide to live with the poor and help them. She founded the Missionaries of Charity in 1950. Since then she has taken care of thousands of sick and abandoned children, given shelter to poor dying people.

Mother Teresa's service to the poor and dying, born out of her love for them, has resulted in many honours and prizes like the Padma Shri (1962), the Nobel Peace Prize (1979) and the Bharat Ratna (1980).

P.T. Usha (born 1964)

India's 'Athletics Queen' as she was known before she retired from the tracks was born in Payyoli, Kerala. P T Usha was national record holder in the 100 and 200 metres and 400 metre hurdles. She represented India at many international track and field events and won gold medals in 100 and 200 metres in Pakistan and silver medals in the same events at the Asian Games, New Delhi in 1982. She also won a gold medal in 400 metre hurdles at the Kuwait Asian meet.

P T Usha participated in the 1980 Moscow Olympics and the 1984 Los Angeles Olympics. She was the first Indian woman to reach an Olympic final. At the 1984 Olympics she qualified for the 400 metre final with a timing of 55.54 seconds and though she bettered this in the final by clocking 54.42 seconds, she finished fourth. She was at her best in Jakarta at the Sixth Asian Track and Field Championships,

Jehangir R D Tata (born 1904)

The Bharat Ratna was recently awarded to the Parsi industrialist J R D Tata for his role in developing modern India's heavy industry. In 1938, he became Chairman of the successful family business which included cotton spinning mills and the huge Tata Iron and Steel Company,

J R D Tata was given "The International Man for 1953" Award for his efforts to create a good relationship with workers in his factories. Today most of the company's huge profits go into education, medical research and social projects. JRD Tata also believes in the capitalist concept of a free-market system for India.

P.T. Usha

Jehangir Ratanji Dadabhoy Tata